THE BOY WITH THE STOLEN VOICE

RAISING A CHILD LABELED WITH "LEARNING DISABILITIES" TO BE WHO THEY ARE IN GOD'S EYES

KAREN MAY

WINNERS
PRESS

Dedicated to …

This book is dedicated to four incredible people who have touched my life in ways that words cannot adequately express.

Heather

To Heather, who has taught me so much through your strength, faith, and hope in God.

Mamasyl

To my dear grandmother Mamasyl, for your unconditional love and unwavering dedication to the care and support of your great-grandson, even in your old age.

Kimberly and Stefan

Lastly, to my beloved children, Kimberly and Stefan, for being the most supportive children who embraced your nephew with such love and patience.

Even a small step forward is a step forward. Celebrate every accomplishment, no matter how small.

— ALEATHEA DUPREE

CONTENTS

THE GOODNESS OF GOD ON TRIAL

"God is good all the time, and all the time, God is good."

This has become one of the most popular church sayings of our time. But is God really good all the time? When tragedy strikes, when bad things happen to good people, when innocent people die suddenly or tragically, or a child is born less than perfect in the eyes of society, sometimes it's the goodness of God that is the first thing called into question. Usually, the first words out of our mouths when tragedy strikes or we're facing a difficult or challenging situation is, "Oh my God!" And sometimes, what starts out as an exclamation of shock or a prayer of desperation ends up becoming an accusation as we begin to wonder, how could a good God allow such a bad thing to happen?

Some years ago, on a bright, chilly, December afternoon around 02:50PM, two school buses, both filled with children, collided as one bus crashed into the side of the other. A forty-six-year-old woman and two little girls, ages six and seven, died in that crash. How could a good God have allowed such a bad thing to happen?

It's a terrible thing to have someone die in an accident, but it's especially painful and strikes close to the heart when a child dies. There's something about tragedy striking an innocent child that causes us to question all that we know and grieves the heart like nothing else. Why do children suffer? Why do they die? Why do they experience disease and life-altering challenges? If anyone deserves to be spared the challenges and calamities of life, shouldn't it be a child?

I've thought a lot about this accident since the day it happened. My heart was so heavy as I thought about the lives of those three precious people that ended here on earth. But as I pondered the details of that accident, the goodness of God filtered through the fog of my grief like slivers of sunlight through a dark cloud. I would like to submit for your review what I call Exhibit A: the school buses involved in the accident.

The buses involved in the accident were 64-

passenger school buses, nearly 11 meters long and weighing nearly 7 tons. That's about 14,000 lbs of mostly steel and glass. It was raining on Tuesday at the time of the accident. Statistics show that a large percentage of vehicle crashes are weather related. They further report that the vast majority of weather-related crashes happen on wet pavement and during rainfall.

It was raining at the time of the accident. The roads were slick, and the accident took place on a busy roadway right at the height of school dismissal traffic. According to reports, the driver of bus #44 made a sharp left turn, crossed the median, crashed into bus #57, and hit it so hard, it turned over on its side. Think of it: one 11-meter long, nearly 7-ton school bus crossed over from one side of the road to the other and crashed into another 11-meter long, nearly 7-ton school bus in the height of busy school traffic on a wet roadway. The fact that no other cars were involved in the collision defies proven statistics for weather-related crashes. Many more people could have been involved in that accident. That's the goodness of God.

Here is something else for your consideration: none of the students on either school bus were strapped in with seatbelts. Keep in mind that one nearly 7-ton school bus slammed into the side of another 6-tonne school bus, and the impact was so hard that one of the school buses turned over completely. Witnesses report that there was a huge *BANG!* The wreckage was so bad that traffic was shut down in both directions, and it took eight hours to clear the accident scene.

Two adults and one child were rushed to the hospital. Twenty other children were rushed to a children's hospital and treated for bumps and scrapes. All were released from the hospital by 9PM that night. That's the goodness of God. Based on how many adults and children reported being treated at the hospital, at least twenty-three other lives could have been taken that day, most of whom were children, none of whom had on seatbelts, yet their lives were spared. That's the goodness of God.

But what about the three lives that were taken: six-year-old Zykia, seven-year-old Seraya, and forty-six-year-old Kimberly? Where is the goodness of God in that? I do not presume to know why their lives weren't spared. Still, I would like to suggest a few possible scenarios for your consideration to point out God's goodness even in the lives of these three people who died in this accident.

Every day, I pored over news articles and watched video recordings to learn more about the lives of the three people who died in this accident. Six-year-old Zykia was described by her mother as a loving, caring, intelligent, and helpful little girl who "never met a stranger." This was Zykia's first year in school, but she was so smart that she was a level ahead of others her age. It was said this little six-year-old girl had the wisdom to match her intelligence. She was described as being full of life, a creative child who loved reading and made bracelets and necklaces to give to her family.

"She loved to go to church," her mother remarked. "I want them to remember her smile."

I see the goodness of God in the life of beautiful, loving six-year-old Zykia.

Seven-year-old Seraya missed the school bus that morning because, according to her mother, she changed outfits so many times she did not make it to the bus stop in time. Her mother suggested she stay home from school that day. Still, Seraya insisted on going because she was so excited about returning her report card to her teacher.

Seraya was described as a happy-go-lucky little girl. She was born prematurely and was hospitalized until she was three months old. But despite the challenges, her family had the privilege of watching her grow into a healthy, happy, and helpful little girl. She had been given the nickname Bubbles even before she was born, and it was said that she was indeed a bubbly and genuinely happy person. Little Seraya was said to light up a room when she walked into it. She was described as an energetic, happy girl who loved school, and most of all, she loved going to church. Her mother urged mourners to be happy and positive like her daughter, Seraya. I see the goodness of God in the life of bubbly, happy, seven-year-old Seraya.

Forty-six-year-old Kimberly was the only adult to die in the accident. She was a teacher's aide and youth minister at her church, and it had been her dream to work in the school system. She was described as having a passion for children, and her life was dedicated to them. That fateful day, Kimberly rode in the seat Zykia's twin brother normally sat in. Had it not been for Kimberly sitting in that seat, Zykia's mother would likely have had two of her children die that day. Instead, her son walked away from the wreckage. Kimberly did not. She died. But as her pastor said, she died where she loved to be the most: among children. I see the goodness of God in the life of dedicated, selfless, forty-six-year-old Kimberly.

WHY I WROTE THIS BOOK

So, what is the point of me sharing all of this, and what does any of it have to do with you and your child? In a word, *hope.* I wrote this book for those who feel lost and have no clue where to start in raising their child. It is for those who feel incapable of raising a child with additional needs and are struggling to see a future for their child. I wrote it because, in your challenging situation, you need hope.

According to the Bible, hope means having an expectation of good. But it is difficult, if not impossible, to have an expectation of good from a God whose goodness is in question. I am not claiming to have all the answers to your questions, but what I have learned, I hope to share with you. Perhaps you will see your journey mirrored in my own.

Mine is a journey that was over twenty-five years in the making. And along the way, I often questioned God's goodness. There were times in my life and in the chronicles of this story when all I saw was despair, hopelessness, and what looked like an impossible situation. But now I can decidedly say, God is a good God.

WHAT YOU WILL GET OUT OF THIS BOOK

As the story of Zykia, Seraya, and Kimberly shows, bad things do sometimes happen to good people. But it also shows us that you can look for the goodness of God even in the most challenging situations you face with your child, and you will find it. Hope in God.

What society interprets as negative circumstances can influence your perspective and undermine your expectation of the goodness of God in your and your child's life. When you feel everyone is judging you and your child by their own idealized standards, this book will help you to rule in favor of the goodness of God. Because God is indeed good all the time, and all the time, God is good.

It is my hope and earnest prayer that as you read my story, you will be more equipped with strategies and find it easier to interact with your child. You will discover the truth about what God says about your child versus what society says. You will learn how to speak words of truth over your child to help shape and groom their life. And you will become confident in your own capabilities and those of your child and fearlessly dream big dreams for your child.

You can find good in any situation, no matter how tragic or challenging. You simply need to look for it.

This is a reality that I discovered through the challenges that I am sharing in this book. Now the goodness of God has become the overarching theme of my life and how I approach every interaction with my child. It is the lens through which I was able to correct and clarify my vision of what society says is true versus what I know to be true based on what I have learned, heard, and experienced. And now, I am sharing these truths with you so you can do the same. Shall we begin?

THE SURPRISE OF EXPECTATION

The sunlight streaming through the window reminded me of the lyrics of a Jimmy Cliff song. It was a bright, sunshiny day. Heather and I were lounging on the settee, chatting about nothing in particular, when she suddenly broke into an unexpected and somewhat girlish grin.

"Guess what?" She paused momentarily to successfully bait me in. "I'm pregnant!"

Her face was beaming, and the heightened excitement overwhelmed her usually reserved personality. We both squealed, bouncing up and down and giggling like schoolgirls, me at the prospect of having a niece or a nephew, and her at having her first child. We were both ecstatic, and Heather could hardly contain herself. She babbled away excitedly, imagining out loud what the baby might be like and making plans for the little one on the way.

She was already three and a half months pregnant when she found out she was expecting. Hard to believe, except for the fact that she was battling systemic lupus and was probably so preoccupied with her frequent flare-ups that the tell-tale signs of pregnancy went unnoticed. Plus, she wasn't expecting to get pregnant. Lupus had robbed her of believing her body was even capable of conceiving. She had no room to carry both a baby and the pain.

We both knew that the pregnancy was risky, but she refused to consider anything but the happiest outcome, and I did not have the heart to say anything that might cast a shadow on her joy. All she knew was that she was pregnant, and she wanted this baby more than anything.

We had always been close, being the last two of four girls. She was older than I was and every bit the bigger sister. We went to college together, became teachers together, celebrated together, but this was by far her greatest accomplishment yet. And, at the time, she desperately needed some good news.

It had been only a year since she was officially diagnosed. Her organs were slowly dying, undetected for years beneath surface skin rashes. Her once glowing, beautiful skin was now ashen and discolored, plagued with open sores that taunted her with healing only to resurface again worse than before. The unwelcome intruder had been given a name, but it had shown its weakness. It shadowed her life like a conjoined twin that could not be separated, but it had not been able to stop the life that was growing inside her. Now, at twenty-seven, the baby she had longed for but never thought she would have was finally on the way.

We talked long into the evening, until the amber hues of a perfect Jamaican sunset cast its golden glow across the airy living room. We were careful to quickly fill in the pauses so there would be no room for doubt to offer its opinion. The Gospel music playing in the background was the perfect accompaniment for reinforcing hope and faith, both of which my sister had in abundance. It was one of the things I admired most about her.

Before the sickness, she was soaring career-wise. She had graduated from college with first-class honors and was doing what she loved: teaching science at one of the major high schools in the area. But slowly but surely, the illness dragged her to the ground, and she had to stop working. After that, everything went downhill.

She did her best to try to keep her spirits up. She insisted on being the life of the party at gatherings; and although she was a bit shy, she forced herself out of her shell and made it a point to be as engaging as possible. She had such great faith, the kind you envied because it seemed invincible and undaunted. Even when she began to have difficulty moving around, she still managed to press her way to attend church services. She believed in fuelling her faith as much as possible. So, it came as no surprise that her stance and security and stability concerning her baby being born safe and healthy were grounded in her trust in God.

Hope is a strange creature. It makes you pray when the sun shines and laugh when it rains. It stubbornly ignores the stone in your shoe as it sets its sights on scaling the mountain before you. It makes the unbearable tolerable. Hope is the engine of faith and the umbilical cord to the future. Realized or unrealized, without it, we would remain victims of diagnoses and prisoners of unfavorable statistics. Hope is not always an expectation of change, but it is the earnest expectation that something good can come out of the worst situations, whether things change or not.

If there's one thing my sister had, it was hope. Heather's optimism burned brightly. Still, it was difficult watching the progression of this monster of a disease, knowing it was ravaging her insides. Her hands and feet were already becoming disfigured, transforming against her will into gnarled extremities as incessant pain wracked her body. But there she sat, glowing triumphantly, convinced that the world was her oyster, and inside it was the pearl of an anticipated birth. She had beat the odds that even healthy women dread. She had made it past the first trimester. Surely this was a sign of good things to come.

2

AT THE BASE OF THE MOUNTAIN

There is nothing quite like growing another human being inside you. There's something magical about the fluttery movements of the first kicks, like little butterflies inside, and watching your entire being transformed day by day into an incubator of potential.

Heather relished every moment of her growing pregnancy. She planned excitedly for the baby, shopping and preparing her home, and looking through books to see which names might best suit this yet unknown personality. She would sit staring at the new crib, imagining the day when it would finally be put to use. And how she longed to kiss those precious little fingers and toes. Most of all, she could hardly wait to hold her little one in her arms and finally look down at the face she daydreamed about. *I wonder if the baby will have my eyes.*

The next two and half months went by quickly, and at six months, the pregnancy took a traumatic shift. Lupus was a jealous occupant and threw cruel tantrums as if protesting the intrusion of another presence in its host. Heather's body started reacting, and as the baby grew, the symptoms of the disease worsened. Her entire body was covered with sores, some of which bore the resemblance and consistency of rotted fruit. And as the flare-ups became more frequent, she could find no peaceful place on her body. At times the flares would be so severe, she needed to be hospitalized for weeks at a time.

It was as though a war was raging inside her body, two entities depending on her for life, one she gladly nourished, the other, like a parasite, depleting her of energy and mobility. It became difficult for her to navigate without feeling pain, and what should have been one of the most joyous experiences of her life was quickly transformed into a challenging journey of pain. Her nervous system was in a state of chaos, and her kidneys and liver had to be checked regularly for fear of failure. The doctors put her on steroids to help reduce the pain and inflammation, but they seemed to only exacerbate her condition.

Her body tried to reject the baby on numerous occasions. But she was strong and remained hopeful, anchoring herself in her faith. No amount of pain could diminish the joy of her baby's arrival. She willed her body to carry the child full-term, but towards the end of her sixth month, her body tired of the fight and ejected the baby prematurely.

Having lupus obviously does not mean you cannot get pregnant, especially if the disease is in remission. However, the presence of symptoms increases the likelihood of complications. If Heather had known she was pregnant, there would have been additional medical intervention and extra monitoring to ensure the early stages of the pregnancy developed as successfully as possible. Early intervention would have helped both the fetus and Heather's body to cope. Instead, her body reacted to the pregnancy as if it were a foreign matter.

The odds were stacked against both her and the baby from the start, and the fact that she was unaware of the pregnancy during those first critical three months was unfortunate. But the early arrival cast only a faint shadow on Heather's joy. Her baby boy had defied the odds and entered the world with all the life and energy his tiny body could muster.

She named him Jonathon, God's gift, and she could not have been happier if God Himself had delivered him to her personally. He was a tiny little bundle weighing less than two pounds. Immediately after birth, the nurses quickly whisked him away and hooked him up to an incubator. That was when Heather's faith fight intensified.

As soon as she could, and as often as possible, she asked to be wheeled to the NICU to see her son. As she peered at his bird-like body through the clear plastic dome of the incubator, the chirps and beeps of the medical equipment served as a constant reminder that there was indeed cause for concern. The fight had not ended at birth. It continued; only the arena had changed.

Jonathon was so small that his respiratory system had not had enough time to develop, and he was struggling to cope. They were both fighting: him outside the womb, and her internally with the disease and the after-effects of the delivery. Still, she managed to put her own suffering aside and focused all of her attention on her son.

When two mountains stand in front of you, you must choose which one you'll climb. You can only climb one at a time, one step at a time. It's so easy to get swallowed up in the what if's or maybe I should haves, but none of that will help you scale the mountain. Worrying is a default response, but no amount of worry will make you any taller. So, you have to look for the nearest crag that you believe will support your weight and heave yourself upward.

Check your gear. What do you have that will help you as you begin your journey? Assess the situation and look for any clefts in the rock where you can ready yourself for the uphill climb. There is nothing at the bottom of the mountain, and it's frightening to stand away from it and look up because the task seems insurmountable. But get closer, examine it closely, and look for the next break.

Heather was still standing firm on her faith, believing that, come what may, Jonathon would be fine. Amidst the daily battery of ongoing tests, she managed to remain hopeful and surprisingly poised in the eye of the cyclone. I was amazed at how at peace she was. Her sweet baby was here, and that's all that mattered. Yes, she was worried, but she did not let that take over. She was sure this baby would survive and would live and be the joy of her life.

3

A QUESTION OF HOPE

Giving birth to a premature baby that you cannot even hold, much less take home, can leave you with a profound sense of disappointment, something akin to shame. There's no bassinet with your child's name on it in the hospital nursery. And when the baby needs milk, instead of the nurses bringing the child to you, you move down the halls of the maternity ward towards the NICU and try not to look to the left or the right at the visitors who may be wondering why your arms are empty. *What's wrong with her? I wonder what happened to the baby?* You presume those are the thoughts of the passers-by who, in your mind, give an awkward smile or look away too quickly.

Jonathon went straight from the womb into the lap of medical intervention. His tiny body was covered in tubes fed into his lungs through his side, nose, and mouth. And there was a laceration at the back of his head from lying on his back for prolonged periods. But this child was a miracle child, kept alive by God's mercy and grace. And he was exactly as his name – a gift!

There were many touch-and-go situations where we thought we had lost him, and then he would miraculously pull through and begin to thrive again. He endured so many different medical procedures, but he survived, and he was a fighter. However, the demands of constant monitoring and support both Heather and Jonathon needed were already becoming overwhelming and constant. Many prayers went up from Heather's church family as well as members of our biological family and friends. Everybody was praying and rallying around her and her husband that this baby would survive. And survive he did.

Jonathon was a fighter. He fought day after day, one strained breath after another, until he pulled through enough to be granted permission to leave the hospital. When the day finally arrived, Heather's heart was so full she could not stop grinning. She would finally be able to take her baby home where he belonged. But when he left, he did not travel alone. He had a constant companion with him everywhere he went: his oxygen tank. The doctors could provide no reassurance about how long he would need it. But it did not matter. Jonathon was coming home!

Leaving the hospital turned out to be the easier part. After she delivered, Heather's body did not go back to her previous normal, if you could call it that. Instead, the lupus became even more aggressive and intensified how it manifested itself. Because the illness was so unpredictable, and because her body reacted so negatively to the pregnancy that wasn't planned for, her condition progressively worsened.

The flare-ups increased to the point that she was not able to really bond with Jonathon. Without the additional help of the NICU nurses, it became even more challenging for her to experience the normal mum-baby bonding and attachment that is so critical for both mother and child. The lupus made it difficult for her to hold Jonathon without experiencing intense pain. Her skin and body were always so sore and tender. She found ways to try to interact with him and do as much as she could for him and with him, but it was *difficult*. She put on a brave face, but inside, only she and God knew how much she was struggling. From time to time, her fear seeped out in words of uncertainty. *I'm not a good mum. How can I take care of my child if I can't even hold him?* Somehow she managed to keep her faith afloat, but her failing body reinforced her feelings of inadequacy.

"I need help!" is one of the hardest things for a parent, especially a new mother, to acknowledge and articulate. It can feel like an admission of incompetence. There you are with this brand-new life that is totally dependent on you for love and care. The scenario is not a novel one because it was that way while the child was growing in the womb. In some ways, it's much easier before the child is born because the care is internal. But after the child is born, and once you leave the cloistered confines of the hospital and round-the-clock dedicated support, the cover is pulled back, and, in your own mind, everyone can see and make their own judgments about how good or capable of a mother you are, or perhaps not.

Many of our fears are exaggerated based on what we *think* others might say or think about our capabilities. A wise person once said, "You would not worry so much about what people thought of you if you realized how little they did." I believe that to be true. However, the fear of how others may react is a pervasive and costly one. It can cause you to misinterpret help as criticism or misjudge support for failure on your part.

Jonathon reached the critical three-month-old milestone with mixed reactions. Heather, of course, was just happy to know her child was growing and continuing to develop. The doctors, however, were starting to express concerns about Jonathon's dependency on oxygen long-term, and the question of how it might affect his brain became a worrisome thought.

But prayers continued, and Heather's resolve was unshakeable. She maintained the hope that Jonathon would pull through with no harmful side effects. In her mind, she was convinced there would be nothing that would negatively impact her child. She was so positive, always laughing and upbeat, even when her body and everything about her was struggling. But what happens when your hope is confronted by the unfeeling facts of medical science? How do you reconcile the two, or can you? These were questions, the answers to which Heather and everyone around her were about to discover.

4

SEARCHING FOR THE DOOR

The joy that filled the house after Jonathon arrived was palpable! This tiny human being became the center of attraction. Every coo, every gurgle, every little movement became a wondrous celebration of this miracle of life we called Jonathon. Before he left the hospital, the doctors advised that they anticipated he would be on oxygen for at least the first eighteen months of his life. So, one of the things we needed to do daily was to keep an eye on his vitals and check things like his hearing and sight.

Since this is my field of expertise, every time I visited Heather, I would do the simple checks you do with babies to make sure they are seeing properly, and their motor skills are functioning normally. I would do the eye-tracking test to see how his vision was and to make sure he was following my fingers and any objects I used. I checked his hearing by banging something loudly, slamming the door, and clapping my hands to see how he reacted, and he was responding perfectly. Heather would watch what I was doing, and both of our faces would light up like Christmas trees every time he passed a test.

Jonathon was developing extraordinarily well, and the entire family couldn't have been happier. We all celebrated when he started walking early. We were overjoyed when he started babbling and then talking early. He was a lively young boy, getting into everything as a toddler does. He ticked every box, and Heather had her perfect, normal baby boy.

As he grew and developed, he started calling Heather mum and using simple words. Aside from his dependency on oxygen, he appeared to be thriving. We rejoiced, convinced that God had heard our many prayers. But when he reached his two-year mark, the house grew silent. There was no more babbling, no more 'mum;' he just stopped talking.

We weren't sure what was happening, so we followed through and got some tests done. That was when my sister received the most devastating news. Jonathon was hearing impaired and diagnosed with autism. The long-term use of oxygen had caused profound hearing loss, and because he could no longer hear, his brain was not getting the stimulation it needed. As a result, he could not process normally, which impacted his speech.

I did not believe he was autistic. I believed his withdrawal was due to a lack of stimulation because his hearing skills had diminished. At that time, autism was just becoming a known thing in our country and a convenient catchphrase. But because it was new, many people did not seem to know about it, so there were not a lot of things in place to address it. Schooling in Jamaica was also not as advanced in the area of developmental challenges at the time, so Jonathon spent just about all of his days at home.

It was hard for Heather because she struggled with coping with her own physical needs and did not accept much of the support offered. She was very stubborn and wanted to prove to herself that she could be the best mum to her son. So she pushed away a lot of the help that could have come her way. She kept saying, "I will take care of him. I will look after him. He's my child. I want him." Still, the pain and disappointment grew. It was almost as if she was grieving silently for her child and grappling with the unspoken fears of her perceived ineptitude in looking after Jonathon and giving him what he needed.

Heather was devastated. She spent quite a bit of her time praying that he would be fine and hoping he would be able to grow out of it, but that hope never materialized. We had enjoyed two years of watching and hearing Jonathon fill the home and our hearts with the joyous sounds only a baby can bring. Then, without warning, it was all cruelly snatched away. It was as though a thief had sneaked in and stolen the very things that brought us the most joy. We would never hear his voice again, and he would never hear ours. Heather felt so broken and so hurt. She was in extreme pain not only because of her illness, but disappointment chewed her up and spit her out, leaving one big question in the place her joy used to be – *why?*

Why was she ill? Why did she have to go through so much pain during her pregnancy? Why was she not able to have a full-term baby? Why did the illness flare up to the point where she could not even interact with her own child? She could not hold him. She could not even so much as touch him because even the gentlest touch from her son's tiny hand would be like setting her skin and body on fire. She just could not do it. But watching her beautiful little boy withdraw deeper and deeper into a world she could not reach, much less enter, was the most difficult pain of all.

It tore me apart to watch my sister suffering like that

and to watch helplessly as my darling nephew slipped further and further away into a distant universe void of sound. It was a struggle. It was a tremendous struggle. We did what many people do when we search for answers and find none, when logic and reason escape us, and we cannot make sense of what we are experiencing. We raise our tear-filled eyes toward the God we trusted when we hoped and prayed and believed all would be well, and with trembling lips we cry out, *Where are You?*

As Heather clutched onto the strings of her faith, mine unraveled. Why would God keep him alive if He knew Jonathon was going to have these issues? The questions crawled out of my mind and infested the crevices of my heart. None of the doctors expected him to live, but he did live. It was a miracle that could only be attributed to God. How could He have saved him, kept him through all of that, only for it to be like this?

My heart ached for Heather. Not only was she struggling with the pain of what she deemed her inadequacies, but, on top of that, the news that her child was profoundly deaf, would never hear again, and might never speak again, tumbled down on her like an avalanche. Heather's blouse was soaked from her tears.

"But we prayed so hard. We *begged* God *so hard!* We asked, and He kept him alive. So, why is this happening now?"

Hot tears streamed down her cheeks as she tried desperately to make some sense out of it all. My gut twisted as I listened to her sobbing. She was beyond consolation. And finding no other scapegoat for all that went wrong, she turned the dagger of blame inward.

"What did I do wrong? Is this some sort of payback for having a child while I was ill? *Is my son being punished because of me?*"

We were both struggling, trying to see God and figure out what role He played in all this. It felt almost like God brought her, and us both, through the wilderness of Jonathon's previous struggles and disappointment and gave us a gift and reward when he was improving. But in light of this recent news, it was almost as if that gift was ripped away from us, especially from my sister's already empty arms. She spent most of her time being ill than not being ill, and then to have this happen. *What happened to the happy ending? If my sister couldn't be well, why couldn't there be at least one happy ending?*

When you find yourself in a pitch-black room, your first instinct is to try to find the door, a way out. The door we were looking for was our faith. We both knew it was still there, but we had to feel our way, slowly groping for hope in the darkness. As if to preserve her own sanity, Heather ultimately convinced herself that

Jonathon would be fine. She rooted herself in the belief that he would indeed eventually grow out of the conditions that restricted him from being able to function the way everyone expected.

It's just a phase. That was the anchor Heather dropped into her ocean of despair. We all wanted to believe – no, *needed* to believe – that his condition would not be forever. And although we were tussling with God, we kept believing Jonathon would hear and speak again.

But the wrestling match with God continued as the years rolled on and there was no kind of improvement. Nothing changed, and after a while, it got even harder to hold onto the belief that things could be different. It was like the slow, suffocating death of hope, and in the final gasps realizing, okay, this is it. There was nothing left to do but accept it and move on. But move on to what? That was the question.

My sister's sense of loss was as profound as Jonathon's loss of hearing as she came to grips with the fact that he would be her only child. And then to realize that he would never be able to do a lot of the things that other children could. It's so easy to take for granted the expectation of having a child who is able to talk and hear your voice. For Heather, the loss was magnified because she could not wrap her arms around her son and reassure him of her love. She could not even bear for him to touch her, and that was a painful and devastating blow.

My visits, which used to be filled with joy and celebration over his development, were transformed into silent observation. Heather and I would just sit and watch Jonathon in his own little world. He would sit by himself, and sometimes he would curl up into a little ball and hug himself. The pain of not knowing his pain was nearly unbearable. There was this sense of utter helplessness. *Now what do we do?*

5

FINDING NORMAL

As Jonathon grew up and got to school age, we got him into a nursery, and again, the level of faith rose. We supposed that maybe when he started nursery, he would see and interact with other children and things would just fall back into place. That did not happen. In fact, being around other children seemed only to compound the issue. He did not even want to engage with them. And the more we watched the dying dream of Jonathon being like other children, the more the sense of powerlessness grew.

He would never be like the other children in Sunday school. He would never grow up to be like the children Heather once taught in school. He would never be like one of the children in our extended family. He would never get there based on how he was presenting.

When I visited Heather at home, I tried to do as much as I could, knowing how difficult it was for her. And even when it seemed like some progress was being made, we knew he needed so much more. It was one thing for us to come to grips with the cold hard facts of Jonathon's condition, but nothing could have prepared us for how others outside the family would react to him. It was extremely difficult watching people look at Jonathon with pity and acting as though deafness was a communicable disease. To them he was alien, something foreign that they did not know how to classify, much less consider as a regular human being. All they could see was a deficient child. But as Jonathon grew, we could see his own unique brilliance emerging.

Despite the challenges, my sister held onto her belief that while Jonathon might not ever be like most other children, he would do well. She believed he had great potential; we all did as a family. And the more we let go of a comparative standard of measurement for normalcy, the more we were able to celebrate his unique gifts and talents.

He loved to play with radios. From as young as age three, he loved taking things apart and putting them back together. With his sense of hearing gone, he keyed into his other senses, and for some reason, he seemed fascinated with lightbulbs. I still can't figure out how he managed to climb the banister, but he would reach the bulb and screw it out. Then he would examine and play with it or just put it somewhere.

Another interesting thing was he seemed to have a keen sense of internal timing. Every evening, just before his dad drove into the driveway, he would grab the bulb, climb back up the banister, and screw the bulb back in. His timing was so precise that, at times, we wondered if he really could not hear.

There were lots of instances where someone would do something or say something, and he would respond appropriately in context. In moments like those, we were sure he was hearing. Those little glimmers gave my sister such hope that there was a possibility that there was some hearing there and that, one day, he would start speaking again. But the diagnosis remained: he was profoundly deaf.

For my sister, the sun rose and set on Jonathon. He was her very heartbeat. Even though he did not speak and he could not hear, he was her pride and joy. She thought the world of him, and nobody could tell her anything different about her son. Yes, he was hearing impaired and unable to speak, but that did not take away his gifts and potential. That's how she saw him, and that's how she celebrated him. She poured into him as much as she could and remained optimistic. As far as she was concerned, his hearing was impaired, but *he* was not.

Heather had big dreams for Jonathon, and she always expected the best for him. Her positivity was infectious and spilled over to the rest of our family. So, rather than focus on what Jonathon could not do, we supported him and celebrated what he could do. He was, indeed, a very clever boy.

Nonetheless, my sister struggled to maintain her positive equilibrium in light of her condition. And as time wore on, she found it increasingly difficult to grapple with the fact that Jonathon was not okay. Admitting that he had some needs that were not within the norm of society's expectations was, to her, like giving up on her son. She refused to accept that he was diagnosed with autism and sometimes insisted that he could hear *something*.

The words "I need help" did not come naturally to my sister. As a result, she spent many years trying to cope on her own, trying to do what she could do. She only accepted the support and help when it was right there in her face. When other family members or I visited, we would help her with Jonathon and herself as much as she allowed us to. She willingly accepted help, but she refused to ask for it. And that was quite hard to see because she was obviously struggling to manage physically. The mental and emotional drain was the worst when Jonathon was young because there was so much going on within her as a person as well.

She still wrestled with feelings of guilt, convincing herself that Jonathon was suffering because of her body and the condition it was in when she was pregnant. We tried to tell her that was not the case, but I don't think she ever accepted that it wasn't her fault. And her feelings of inadequacy as far as taking care of her child caused her to push away all the help that could have benefited Jonathon and herself.

She continued to question God.

"Why can't I just be able to hold him and hug him. I want to."

And the more she tried to do it, the more her disappointment grew. With every failed attempt, she grew more despondent and even more obstinate. It was as though she needed to prove to herself that she could be a good mum. But the standard she set was her own. In my eyes, she was a good mum. She kept Jonathon despite the challenges they both faced. She kept him clean and fed – to this day, I still marvel at how she did it. But her unanswered questions of how this could happen became as chronic as her illness, and the emotional torment took its toll.

Heather's life became a continuous cycle of hospital

admissions and discharges as her body seemed to reject all the medication. Hurt, pain, and disappointment slowly poisoned her positivity, leaving her with a mixed bag of emotions. She spent most of her days cooped up at home with this young child who needed so much more than she was capable of giving. It reached a point where she seemed stuck in an endless loop, trying to solve it all on her own and get it right. But the problems she was facing were too big for her to fix.

It was hard to watch. It was even harder to know that I could help, but she could not bring herself to ask for the help I could provide because she wanted to show everybody that she was capable of being Jonathon's mum. She wanted to be the person to offer him what he needed. And although she knew there was no way she could possibly manage all the care he needed on her own, she refused to accept it. There was also an underlying fear that if she was deemed incompetent, there might be a risk that Jonathon would be taken away from her. So she plowed through and plodded on, rejecting help and rejecting support beyond the bare minimum.

Denial can masquerade as hope and pride for self-sufficiency. Overcoming these is sometimes much more difficult than the medical challenges being faced. Initially, the shock of a diagnosis you weren't expecting can throw you into denial. But persistent denial can be birthed from the comparison of what you have and what you believe you should have. Such comparisons may be unfair to the uniqueness of the child you have been given. Normal is conforming to the typical, and your child is anything but that.

Pride is the most resistant to progress. Pride is the lie you believe about yourself, and inadequacy is a flawed measurement based on standards that don't amount to much in the grand scheme of things. Help is help, whether it comes from you or others who care about you and your child. Accepting the help you need is not a sign of weakness or an admission of your inability to cope. It is the willingness to do whatever it takes so that you *can* cope. And there is nothing shameful about that. Anything that suggests otherwise is a lie.

6

TIPPING THE SCALE

During the times my sister was in the hospital, my grandma, who was also a teacher, took on most of Jonathon's care. We banded together as a family and held to our views that Jonathon could do just about anything anyone else could as long as he had the right support and input. The views of others were mixed though. So, as a family, we had to be even more intentional about being positive and proactive in treating Jonathon as a unique human being who needed extra support. Other people, however, were not as understanding.

Jonathon's deafness seemed to push people outside the family to the limit of what they deemed acceptable. In their minds, they could not see any usefulness in him. He was deaf and not talking, so to them, there was not much he would get out of school, interaction, or life itself. When most people discovered he was hearing impaired, their default response was to simply ignore him as if he did not exist. The deafness they might have barely tolerated, but the fact that he could also not speak was too much for them to deal with.

A lot of times, they did not verbally say anything; however, their attitude towards Jonathon and how they interacted with him spoke volumes. Beyond the perfunctory awkward smile, most people did not speak to him at all. They might speak about him, or around him, but rarely directly to him. It was almost as though because he was not hearing or speaking, there was nothing else about him they felt was worth acknowledging.

At school, it was more of the same. They put Jonathon in a box and settled in their minds that this was as good as it would get, so no need to do anything over and above the bare minimum. They did not deem it necessary to go the extra mile to see what he was capable of as they might a hearing child. Instead, they adopted the attitude that whatever task he was given, if he did it, he did it. And if he did not do well, of course, the only possible explanation would be that he did not hear and could not speak.

The views of others, whether positive or negative,

greatly impacted Heather. The negative views increased her sense of loss, hopelessness, and helplessness. Her dream, her heartbeat, the child she had yearned for so many years was now a child that was not deemed worthy of most people's time or efforts. And he was often written off as a hopeless case. At the other end of the pendulum, the positive views helped her to maintain her faith and hope for Jonathon to enjoy life as a human being should and do the best he could with the gifts and talents he had.

At times, it was difficult to watch and listen to people interact with Jonathon because I know how much what people think about a person can impact what they do, who they become, and whether or not they grow and develop or stay stuck. The varied reactions to Jonathon bounced between awkward silence and "Oh, poor thing." The consensus bought into what society thinks about children who have limitations from different conditions or sensory issues.

A disability simply means there is a part of the body that causes a limitation to what is seen as the norm. Jonathon's ears and voice were not functioning, so to some, he was not good or worthy enough to be counted among "normal" people. They would pity him, and if they felt generous, they would give him the basics, but that was it.

I can't tell you how many times we walked into a room full of people, and they would greet everyone except Jonathon. Or they would say, "Hi, Jonathon," and then fuss over him without much expectation of a response. If a rare person was in a magnanimous mood, they might try and talk to him. But when he does not respond, they walk away. It would often give the impression that it was a waste of energy to even try to engage with him any further.

When you think about it, people often interact for their own gratification. For example, people will have entire conversations with newborns whose only responses may be infant reflexes. Or they might talk to a dog that wags its tail or barks. As long as there is a response that makes the person feel satisfied that they have been heard and in some way acknowledged, they will continue. But interaction for the benefit of the person being spoken to is not the standard of communication.

Jonathon was, in large part, ignored by society. To most, he was not worth their time and effort. He was not worth the investment of being given much because he was not giving back to them. So, the attitude was more or less, *why should we bother?* And this mindset was displayed in all forms and aspects of society. School was almost like a tick-box exercise. The law said Jonathon needed to be in school, so he was enrolled and labeled as a child with learning disabilities and autism. Then, because he had those labels, the school system would automatically lower the bar or remove it altogether. *This is who he is. He can't hear or speak, so don't expect much.* Consequently, much was not poured into him. Much was not given to him, because if you do not expect much, you will not give much.

It was like a distorted reversal of a scripture in the Bible that says, to whom much is given, much is expected. As far as a person with disabilities like Jonathon was concerned, the standard is, to whom less is given, less is expected. The school system did not expect much from him, so they did not pour into him. Society as a whole treated Jonathon differently than a child who did not have any of his limitations; they are poured into, and he is not. But, to me, that's like cheering to encourage the child who usually kicks the winning goals rather than cheering to encourage the child who can barely make contact with the ball. Shouldn't the one who needs the most encouragement also be encouraged?

The general rule of society is if a person has a limitation or something that stops them from looking like they are a part of the norm, they are ostracized and pushed to the periphery of acceptability. They are given the basics as human beings – food, clothing, shelter – but that's where it stops.

Where do the boundaries of "limitation" start and end? Jonathon is a human being. His ears and voice do not work the way we might expect, but he has a brain. He's clever; he understands what you say. Granted, he may not have the ability to express that he understands as quickly as most do. But if you took the time to make sure you're speaking and communicating with him so that he clearly understands, and then took the time to allow him to respond to you, whether through body language, pictures, or whatever else could be used, his abilities to communicate would be evident.

However, that is not usually the case. That takes too much time, patience, and kindness for most. So, society treats children like Jonathon as if he is less than human, less than them, less than who God intended them to be. Yes, they have limitations, but we all do in one way or another, whether they be obvious, like Jonathon's, or not.

Society's estimation of Jonathon's abilities was difficult to accept. Heather, as a parent, and I, as a relative, could see a child who has so much to give but isn't allowed to give because he is labeled, caged in, and then literally blocked from developing. That magnifies the sense of loss for a parent or relative because there is nowhere else to go. We live in society, and so we must function within the parameters of its laws and systems. But what do you do when the systems that should be in place to help children like Jonathon adopt the same "that's as good as he'll get" attitude? If you are not careful, the views of others and society help solidify and cement a sense of loss: the loss of dreams, of lost hope, and the loss of expectations for your child. That can become part of an "expect nothing or nothing much" mindset.

As a teacher, Heather knew what it meant to pour into a child and help that child grow, and she could not do that. And the system she had expected to do it and had been a part of failed miserably. It failed her and her child.

Every parent or guardian of a child with disabilities must contend with a balancing act. You are forced to balance what you see versus what the world sees. At the beginning of your journey, the scales will undoubtedly be tipped in favor of what society deems "normal" for your child. But for your child to have a fighting chance in this world, *you* must tip the scales.

Tip the scales in favor of their uniqueness by celebrating who they are rather than who society says they should be. Tip the scales by constantly testing the limits of their abilities rather than accepting the limitations imposed upon them by systems that refuse to raise the bar to the level of their possibilities and potential. And when a boundary in what they are capable of doing has been reached, do not grieve what they could not do. Instead, celebrate what they can do.

A child with disabilities is still a human being. They have bodies, hearts, gifts, and talents, and need to be nurtured just as all human beings need to be nurtured. Jonathon is a gift from God. He is a miracle child, and he was created by God like everyone else. The negative estimations of society do not define him. And the support of those of us who love him is a critical factor in determining his quality of life, as we were about to discover.

7

THE TRANSITION

There came a point in Heather's life where the cry for help was no longer optional. Her health was quickly deteriorating to the point where her extremities were affected. She faced the likelihood of losing a limb and not being able to take care of Jonathon at all. The lupus flared out of control, and the doctors threw their hands up, exasperated that they had exhausted their medical knowledge and resources. There was nothing more they could do to help her. She was left with only two options: stay in Jamaica and let her body die piece by piece, or leave the country in search of a chance at survival.

After many tears and prayers, Heather made the heart-wrenching decision to go to America to continue treatment. As much as it pained her to leave her son, her prized possession, who she loved more than anything, it was her only hope. She wanted to be there for him and watch him as he grew up to become the outstanding person she knew he had the potential to become. But separating from him was the only way she could have a shot at securing more time.

Jonathon was only eight years old when his mum left. By then, I was already living in the United Kingdom, so the only person she could leave Jonathon with was our grandmother. Of course, Heather put on a brave front, assuring herself and us that she would not be gone for long. But "not long" turned into a year, then two years, and two years became four. Then in May 2008, Heather became adamant about having Jonathon join her in America, and plans were made to that end.

It is said that, sometimes, just before a person dealing with a chronic illness or terminal disease dies, their condition seems to go into remission. Suddenly, they seem to have a spark of life and hope that a miracle has taken place. Heather's request to see Jonathon and have him near her was that spark of life. Like a marathon runner making that last push to victory, her faith surged. But her movement was upward rather than forward, and her wish to see the son she loved so much was not to be granted. She passed away two weeks before he was to join her in the USA.

In the months that followed, I was engulfed by grief at the loss of my sister and carried the weight of her unrealized request to see her son. Could it be she had an inkling she was dying and wanted to see him one last time? Those of us who remained had no way of knowing how Jonathon was affected by the death of his mother. Surely, as heightened as his senses had become, he was at least aware that there was one less person in the room or in the house. But I could not help but wonder if he knew she was gone for good. Was there a memory somewhere deep in the recesses of his mind that, once upon a time, he had heard her voice? Was there a sensory memory of her sacrificial touch or the warmth of her breath as she spoke words he could no longer hear? Was he aware that a bright light was no longer shining within his reach?

I had always promised Heather that if anything happened to her, I would take care of Jonathon and raise him just as if he were my own child. In the years and months before my sister's death, I had broached the sensitive subject of taking Jonathon and looking after him. He was growing up so fast and was more than a handful for my grandmother to take care of the way he needed to be taken care of. But Heather refused. The hope of being able to one day raise her child herself was her lifeline, and she could not let go. She did the best she could – her very best. But when she died, there was no one else in Jamaica to take care of him, so I gladly took him as my own.

Jonathon was eleven when his mum died. She died in June, and by September, just as summer transitioned into autumn, Jonathon came to the UK to live with my family and me. I wasted no time getting full parental responsibility through the courts and got everything in place so he could be properly taken care of. And Jonathon officially became my child – my son.

It was as though when my sister transitioned, she released all the love she had in her heart for Jonathon and bequeathed it to me, bestowing me with the grace to love him for her in her absence. He became so much a part of my family and my world that I almost felt like I had given birth to him myself. Heather's aspirations and ambitions for Jonathon's future became my own. And all the love Heather wanted to give him flows through my heart to him, along with my own love for him, which makes him twice loved.

Jonathon's addition to our family was easier for some than others. My own two children were quite young at the time: my daughter was six years old, and my son was about eighteen months. The children, being so young, took the adjustments in stride. Initially, the whole family, including my husband, was excited about his coming. But it did not take long for the stress of Jonathon's daily care and support to put a strain on my marriage. There was some tension and disagreements between my then husband and me that affected the family as a whole. So, things did get a little bit rocky shortly after Jonathon arrived.

When Jonathon came to us, he had to get acclimated to a new country and a climate that was physically and socially a very different experience from what he would have had in Jamaica. We also had to get acclimated to him being part of our nuclear family. My early interactions with him were a bit strange at first. It was like getting to know your child who had been separated from you for years. Since he could not speak or hear me, I had to find other ways to connect with him. I did a lot of observation to understand his body language, his gestures, how his mind thinks, and what he liked and disliked. I literally had to learn everything about him from scratch, the way I learned about my birth children as they were growing up.

Things I would take for granted and do naturally with my other two children required a little more forethought with Jonathon. Sometimes, I had to take a completely opposite approach with Jonathon than I would my own children because he did not speak or hear. Interacting with people with disabilities was something I did professionally. That was and is my passion and life, so it was easier to start interacting with him. But I quickly discovered that having to do that on a continuous basis every day was very different. There was no time when I was "off the clock." Jonathon was my son now, and he needed a lot of love and reassurance as I learned how best to communicate with him and he with me.

At times, caring for him was very challenging. However, maintaining the view that Jonathon was just like my other children, but just needed extra support and interaction, made it easier for me to cope and kept me from focusing on the negatives. As a family, we did not adjust our behavior to his limitations. Instead, we treated him like any other member of the family and gave him the opportunity to adjust to our normality. So, we did everything as a family. We ate together. We had fun together. We went out together. We went on holidays together. And Jonathon rose to the occasion and learned how to fit into the family.

Interestingly enough, because we treated him no differently from anyone else in the family, other people reacted to that. We did not make a fuss about what he could or could not do. So people who were around us more often and got to see how we treated Jonathon, learned not to make a fuss either. He went to church with us and was part of our church family as much as the rest of us. Nevertheless, there were painful moments when someone would take it upon themselves to point out that Jonathon was not like my other children. Yes, I recognized that. I acknowledged that he was not like my daughter or my other son. But by the same token, I also acknowledged that my daughter and youngest son were not like Jonathon. They are different, and that's okay.

You see, how we respond to or interpret the comments and opinions of others – careless and callous as they might be – is often a matter of your own perspective. For example, if someone said my daughter is not like my youngest son, I would not mind because there would be no perceived inference of abnormality, just a noted difference. So, it boils down to what I know and believe about my child, not what anyone else says. Understanding that helps take the sting out of thoughtless remarks.

Integrating Jonathon into our family as my son was a learning curve for everybody. It was a way for us to expand our repertoire of how to deal with a unique individual who does not fit neatly into what mainstream society calls "normal." He brought out the best in us because we had to dig deep to be more patient and understanding, and to take the time to really observe what makes Jonathon so unique. In that sense, he helped us to be more human.

Getting to know Jonathon caused me to realize how lackadaisical we, as human beings, can be in our interactions with others. We tend to take so much for granted that we rarely take the time to appreciate the uniqueness of another human being. That is until we encounter someone – maybe someone like Jonathon – who forces us to slow down and appreciate who they are as a unique individual.

Jonathon changed me for the better simply by being who he is. I began to realize areas where I needed to improve, things I took for granted before he came. I gained a greater understanding of the nuances of what human beings are and do. His presence in our lives strengthened my resolve that everybody has a right to be who they uniquely are, no matter what labels are put on them or what conditions they have.

Nonetheless, juggling a full-time job, managing Jonathon's care with two very young children also needing my attention, plus a husband, and trying to make everything work was extremely difficult. So, I had to ask for help. Fortunately, getting the support I needed was easier because the systems in England were much better than in Jamaica. However, the actual help, and the quality of it, was and is sometimes questionable.

I did not have any other relatives in the UK, but I had a best friend who became like a sister and was very supportive. I could also get help through the school system or a social worker. And the care system provided what they call respite care, which is designed to provide the caregiver with breaks from caring. But therein lies the problem. How do you take a break from caring? It's really not possible. So, although the system is designed to give you a break, it isn't really a break because you are constantly overseeing and making sure the child is being treated as they should be.

Because of my field, I knew how and where to ask for help, but the help I could find was somewhat restrictive. I found myself facing some of the same limitations Heather had faced when dealing with professionals and systems of care. There were different support systems and networks, for example, the National Children's Deaf Society and other organizations like that. But I found the information was sometimes so general or so generic that it was not useful. Everybody was put in the same pot, and it was very hard to find information that was not stereotypical.

There were sometimes a lot of barriers to getting help because people often had their own ideas about what they thought Jonathon needed. I quickly discovered that opinions are like bellybuttons:

everybody has one. Each professional would have their own ideas about what Jonathon needed and were unwilling to entertain any other helpful recommendations they deemed outside the realm of their expertise. So, the help was fragmented and disjointed.

Finding help became a juggling act trying to balance a multiplicity of ideas, opinions, explanations, and systems. I found the help offered to be majorly tokenistic: more a matter of words than personalized actions. But I wanted Jonathon to be treated like a human being and not just another nameless care recipient in a system that only recognized issues but not individuality.

Help is not helpful unless it's helpful. Instead, it becomes another stressor and makes your job as a parent much harder. One of the things I've found as Jonathon's parent is the dichotomy of wanting to listen to what the professionals have to say, but at the same time, knowing what my child needs and yet being refused to be heard. I live with Jonathon every day. I know the ups and downs; I've got inside information. And it's sometimes difficult to explain that point of view to someone who has no personal experience with my child and is just doing their job.

Support for a child who is dealing with issues like

Jonathon's should not be a mutually exclusive endeavor. But more times than not, that is the approach taken. It is as if the system trains professionals to adopt the attitude that says to parents or carers, *you keep all your helpful information to yourself, and let me do my job.* But I know my child well enough to know the support he needs, and it's challenging when the various professionals tell you something different.

The balancing act never works because it just makes life more stressful. You become more anxious, and you actually start feeling a sense of distrust for the system that is supposed to be helping you. But, at the same time, if you don't take their advice and something happens, that could make it harder for the child and you.

The only way I've found to deal with this dilemma is to flip the script. Instead of pushing what I know about the needs of my child to the background and building a plan of action based solely on the opinions of the professionals, I use what I know about my child and his needs as the foundation for the help I'm seeking. Then I use my knowledge to undergird the advice and recommendations of the professionals. In other words, I acknowledge that I am the expert in my child's care. With that as the basis, I network whatever auxiliary help is needed for my child's best interests.

I understand how draining it can be as a parent of a

young person who requires a lot of extra support. I know how tempting it is to decide you're not going to balance anything and go with whatever the professionals say. There will be days when you will just want to get on with life as best as you can. But you have to be strong, clear-minded, and focused as a parent. You cannot afford to be passive about the needs of your child and simply go along with the generic order of the day. You have to know what you want, what your child needs, and be willing to voice it and keep voicing it.

8

TILTING PERSPECTIVES

We are each given our own eyes through which to view the world. Despite how perceptive we may be, we were never given the ability to actually see through someone else's eyes. That's for a reason. We have the gift of seeing the world through our own eyes and looking at our children through our own eyes. But society's perception of what they see as "different" or "disabled" is from a skewed perspective. None of it is based on authentic and pure interaction. Instead, it has been jaded by negativity and presumption. But you have the opportunity to focus on and nurture the wonder of who your child is as a unique human being, not "different from" in a negative sense, or "less than," but uniquely them.

There's a verse in the Bible that poses a question

worthy of our consideration: does the creation get to say to the Creator, "Why did you make me this way?" Part of what makes life with a uniquely-abled child easier is resolving that question in your own mind. When we look at other created things, even things that might make us uncomfortable because they are so different from our everyday reality, we are able to accept their uniqueness. Take the animal kingdom, for example. We might not particularly care for what a hippopotamus looks like, but we still see it as a thing of wonder and have some sense of appreciation for how it was made. We may not like what we see, but we never judge them. We do not compare them to other species of their kind. We simply accept that is how they were meant to be. We should be able to extend the same courtesy to human beings, and even more so.

I needed to resolve this question of differentness and look at my new son for who he is. What makes him tick? How does he respond to the world around him? How does he express his human nature? How does he speak to me? If he does not or cannot speak to me as other human beings do, does that make him any less of a human being? Although he does not have speech, he still has a voice. He has body language, expressions, moods, and emotions. The only thing that was different was how he expressed those emotions because of who he is. But isn't that true of all of us?

People may say, "he's not like others," but that statement needs to be challenged. Is it hearing and speech that makes us like others? Suppose I was the only English-speaking person in a room full of people from other countries who all spoke different languages and could only understand me through an interpreter. Would I deem their humanness different from mine? If speech and hearing were the only distinguishing factors of our humanness and alikeness, we would be greatly disadvantaged in our appreciation of the vast diversity among our species.

So, what do I do when confronted with people and systems that seem determined to create a line of division between them and anyone who they perceive as unlike them? I keep loving my child, and I love him the same as my other children who do not share his conditions. What do I do? I learn how to understand him and help him to learn how to understand me and others with whom he is familiar. I demonstrate what acceptance and belongingness feel like by loving him without any conditions. And I release him from any expectations that he has to be, look, or act a certain way. In short, I treat him like the wonderful, unique human being he is.

Nobody is like the other. We each have our own

unique way of seeing and doing things. We have our own way of expressing ourselves and interpreting the expressions of others. And Jonathon – and others like him – are no exception. He has gifts and talents. At times, he struggles, as do we all. And all struggles are an opportunity to acknowledge where we need to exercise our own character. So, rather than pointing out what he cannot do, I take the time to identify what he would be able to do if I invested more time, energy, and effort. It's not my responsibility to make him like others. Instead, it is my privilege to help him be uniquely him, with all that involves.

So, do I settle for what the systems and professionals, and society as a whole decide, or do I push for the potential I see in my child? No, I'm not settling. To do so would be to rob Jonathon of his voice entirely. Right now, I am his interpreter, the liaison between him and the rest of the world. His language may not be native to my own, but I have taken the time to learn it and become fluent in it.

Everyone needs the right support to achieve anything in this life. So do not settle for what strangers and systems decide. Instead, push for what you believe your child needs. Fight for the things that will give them a better quality of life and a chance to develop as a person, to succeed, and reach their fullest potential. If left to the system, Jonathon would become just another statistic. He would be labeled with a learning disability and written off as someone who is incapable of achieving anything. He would be resigned to needing a high level of support for the rest of his life. So, I cannot settle, because settling would mean I believe the confining stereotypes relegated to him by the systems that refuse to adequately support him.

The system starts from the standpoint of helping someone like Jonathon be "good." But I do not need to help him to be good because he is already good. That shift in perspective changes everything. It is no longer about "fixing" Jonathon and trying to get him as close as possible to what society thinks he should be. Instead, the focus is placed on helping to bring out the best of what is inside him. That required me to learn to put into practice what I preached as part of my profession, and I did. I went the extra mile. I invested more time and effort. I literally pushed him to be and do what I knew he had the capacity to do without any excuses, caveats, or boundaries. That is no less than what I would do for any of my children.

So, he learned how to make his own breakfast. He learned how to spread his own bed and help keep the house clean. He learned how to fold his clothes and use the washing machine. I knew if I had listened to what the medical and educational professionals said, I would have limited him. So, pouring into him, investing time, and having a clear vision and a clear understanding of who Jonathon uniquely is, was key to helping him get to where he is today. I refused to make excuses and enable what society thought he could not do unless I had proved he had reached his limit in a particular area of capability.

All of us are human beings. We all have flaws and failures. We may not be classified as learning disabled, but each of us has our own limitations. So, I can never settle for what "they" decide Jonathon cannot be or cannot become. He *can* become and be with the right input and support. I know who my child is in the sight of God. Therefore, I know that he is able to do all things through Christ who strengthens him. And for me, as his mother standing in the gap, I too can do all things through Christ who strengthens me to help him.

So, I had to learn how to engage with professionals to be able to help him and challenge the ceilings people put in place for him. I had to learn how to stand up on his behalf because he could not speak for himself. It's up to me to teach others what I know and see and have envisioned for him. It's an opportunity to help them to come on board and understand that he can learn if given the same opportunities as others who are not labeled with a condition or disability.

My views are different because I am extremely positive about the lives people who are labeled with disabilities can lead. As for Jonathon, I can be his voice. I can be the measuring stick of what others are expecting of him. I can show others his goodness and point out the positive things he can do. I can also point out the things that are not true, things that have been spoken or attached to Jonathon that are not valid or justifiable because he sits outside of their predefined box and set of rules. Not being able to hear or speak does not limit him from processing. He processes differently, but my daughter processes differently from my other son, and he processes differently from her. So who am I – or anybody – to then say that because Jonathon is hearing impaired and does not speak he is different, or he can't learn, or he can't process?

I realized I had to change how I then presented myself and presented him. I asked myself what can I do? What difference can I make? How can I help others understand and see that he has everything inside him that he needs? It's just how we support him, how we interact with him, and how we encourage him. The expectations that we have often make the biggest difference.

I had to decide if I would be someone who accepted what was being said about Jonathon and just leave it to chance that he would be okay, or if I would be his voice. Would I stand up for him and fight and let people know who he is and what he can do? Would I celebrate him and make sure his life is not reduced to people feeling sorry for him? Would I try to tilt the perspective of those who see him as not being productive or useful? I had to. I had to make a stand as his parent and refuse to settle for anything less than his best.

Not settling requires courage because you're up against a system that is mandated to provide a certain high level of support. It could end up being detrimental to the child if they think you are not doing what they want you to do, or you're not seeing things their way. Make no mistake about it: there could be negative repercussions for not settling. However, as a parent, you have to know deep in your heart – deep within you – that what you see for your child and in your child is the right thing. And if you believe and *know* that, then the battle is worth fighting.

Admittedly, there were times I was tempted to give up and just kind of let things slide because it was so hard. It is difficult trying to live your life while at the same time splitting yourself between all the people who depend on you. This is especially true if you have other children and other interests. On top of that, having to fight against decisions that you know are not the best can be draining. It can be tiring and make you feel almost helpless because the systems meant to help you are often the ones that fight against you and your child. But I refuse to give up. I'm convinced the battle is worth fighting.

Giving up is not an option. There is no Plan B. Negotiate if you must, but stand on what you believe and insist on getting the right support and network around you to help you on your journey. There are variations of support, some positive, some negative, and some a combination of the two. It all depends on who you're dealing with and where the support comes from. But it is up to you to determine whether those who are offering support have an honest view of your child or if they are putting your child in a box.

If you settle for labels and stereotypes, you will be stuck with generic support and lower expectations. There are no easy answers. It's a hard journey. Nevertheless, it's one that can be done with faith, hope, and a clear vision of yourself as a parent. Without a doubt, it's a journey that is worth taking, and you *can* do it.

9

THE TURNING POINT

The smoke detector chirps in the background. The battery needs changing. I stand there quietly observing, not wanting to disturb the moment. Jonathon is seated at his favorite spot at the table with jigsaw puzzle pieces spread out in front of him. His concentration is intense as he busily shifts the pieces around until he finds what he's looking for. Another match. He can beat anyone in the family putting puzzles together in no time. It takes us twice or thrice as long to do what he does in record time. He's absolutely brilliant when it comes to creating things and putting things together. One of the many things he can do that others in the family cannot.

I look at his handsome face and shadowy beard and

can hardly believe fourteen years have gone by since he first came to us. Tears fill my eyes as I think of Heather. *He's all grown up now!* I'm overwhelmed with emotion as I think back on the many improvements in his life over the years, and my heart nearly bursts with pride.

My mind drifts back to my childhood when I was about seven. There was a boy in my neighborhood who had down syndrome who became my best friend. At the time, the term 'down syndrome' was not yet popularized, and people with down syndrome were referred to as retarded or mongoloid. For some reason, I was drawn to people who were different.

I also remember a lady in our community who had seizures or fits, as we referred to the condition back then. When she had seizures in the town center, around the neighborhood, or even along the roadside, I would wriggle my way through the crowd and watch with keen and concerned interest. I took note of how people reacted to her, and I felt a strange attachment to her. After an episode, I would talk to her when others shied away from her as if her seizures were contagious.

From those early years, I knew I wanted to work with people who were different. When I got to college, the only option I considered as far as a specialty was teaching people with disabilities. I finished my teaching diploma in 1994. Little did I know, at the time, that this passion I had for working with people with disabilities would prepare me for something that would be even dearer to my heart. Three years later, Jonathon was born.

People with disabilities deserve to be treated with the same worth and value as every other human being. I've believed this for as long as I can remember. Then when I had the privilege of taking Jonathon into my family, I truly realized that he is no different from any of us. The same way I had to teach my two children different things is the same way I had to teach him. It took a bit longer for him to learn some things, and I may have had to repeat myself, but that was no different from repeating myself with my other two children who were not labeled in any way.

A major turning point was when I got to experience interacting with Jonathon on a daily basis, and then watching him grow and develop skills that other people thought he would never develop. That really reinforced everything I felt before about the value and worth of people who are labeled and people who are not given chances. But the thing that really cemented my perspective was when I had a talk with God.

I was sitting in my room, quietly reflecting on the blessings in my life and expressing my gratitude to God. I thought about the overwhelming passion I have to change how people view children and young adults with disabilities, and a question that had been resting deep in the recesses of my heart bubbled up to the surface.

"What do *You* think about Jonathon and others like him, Lord? How do *You* see them?"

There's not much in the Bible about disabilities or anything that would indicate what God thought about people who are disabled. As I sat quietly waiting for His response, God started downloading His view with a still, small voice inside my heart.

"I came for everyone," He said.

I could already feel the tears starting to well up. I remained quiet as He continued.

"*They* are part of the '*everyone.*'"

His words reverberated in my heart: *they are part of the "everyone."*

After giving me a few moments, as if to absorb what He had just said, He continued.

"They need to hear Me; they need to learn about Me. I don't see them as disabled or anything less than anyone else. I see them as being wonderfully and beautifully made in My image."

Grateful tears flowed freely as the impact of those words penetrated my heart. All the promises and blessings and everything God has for the human race which He created is what He has for people like

Jonathon who have been ostracized, labeled, and pushed into a corner. From that moment, whenever I looked at Jonathon, all I could see was how much God loves him and us. Jonathon was made in His image, and everything God thinks about human beings, He thinks about my child. God is not concerned about labels of intellectual issues or other disabilities. He sees my child and others like him as wonderfully and beautifully made, no different from any other human being.

It was the most profound affirmation of what I believed in my heart to be true all along. It changed my view even more radically about what my child can do, what he can achieve, and the potential he has. So, if God says my child is beautiful, then he is beautiful. If God's view is that my child is gifted and talented, that remains my prevailing view no matter what any institution, medical professional, or statistic says.

God boosted my expectations for my child and bolstered my belief that everything that is available for everyone else is available for my child. Using a principle I learned from the Bible about calling things into existence that do not exist, I started to speak into my child's life even more. I began to call healing into this life. And although his hearing is not totally restored, I've seen signs of improvement, especially in the way he tries to express himself.

God constantly reminds me to verbally affirm who He says my child is. So, every day, I speak words of affirmation over him:

My child is not less than. He is worthy of everything that he can have or should have. He is the head and not the tail. He is successful. He is the apple of God's eye. He is healed, saved, and everything God says he is. He's talented, brilliant, and smart. He's a work of art – a masterpiece!

Everything God calls my child, I call my child. And what is true for him is also true for you and your child.

I will keep on fighting for Jonathon, I'll keep speaking into his life, and I'll also keep letting others know that it is not acceptable to think anything less of him than who he is. He is supported by care workers, but they literally treat him as if he's an idiot. They act like he's an imbecile who has no sense, can't think, and can't do anything for himself. So I have to keep reminding them who he is and what he can do. I have to keep teaching them and modeling for them how to treat and interact with Jonathon. I constantly tell them to stop looking at what they think Jonathon *can't* do and look at what he *can* do. He can do so many things, but they limit him because they think he cannot.

For example, I've watched on many occasions as carers struggle with Jonathon's bag and allow him to walk away with his two hands in his pockets. I send them back with the bag every time. They look at me as though I'm being mean or unreasonable, but I simply look at him and tell him, "You have two hands; go and do what you need to do."

It's almost amusing to watch the expressions on their faces when he takes his bag and does what he needs to do with it. They are always so surprised. Why? Because they came in with a preconceived idea that he could not do it. They look at me in wonder and exclaim, "Wow! How do you get him to do that?" I explain to them that I get him to do that because he knows what I think of him. He understands the expectations that I have of him, and he knows what he can do. He knows he won't get away with not doing something because that's not how we see or treat him. So, it is my responsibility as his parent to let them know who he is, and their responsibility to help him become even more of who he is.

Keep rooting for your child. Keep ensuring that other people see them the way God sees them. It is said that you teach people how to treat you by what you allow, what you stop, and what you reinforce. Since your child cannot teach those who care for him or teach him in the school system, you must do it for them. Insist that those who work with your child help them to fulfill the potential that is in them. Because without your input and expression of that expectation, they will treat your child as if they are not good enough and, consequently, stifle their potential rather than help them fulfill it.

I have a lot of faith in what Jonathon can achieve, but faith without works is dead. If I don't put in the work to help him make those achievements, he might never achieve them. I've been able to celebrate so many of his accomplishments and who he has become. I put myself in the position to make sure I'm rooting for him and building him up. He is, after all, one of my greatest and most prized investments. If I don't do it, who will?

Those of us who have not been classified as disabled have the world at our feet. We freely pursue our education; we are encouraged to pursue personal development, but very few make those kinds of opportunities available for young people with disabilities. They are not seen as worthy or worth it. And it's not just people with disabilities who get treated this way. Children who are labeled because they have bad behaviors are also often viewed as less than. They're not less than. It's the expectations people have of them that are less than. As a result, their lives are not deemed worthy of investing in. Few see them the way God sees them, and so it's difficult for them to see themselves that way. And similar to Jonathon and others like him, their abilities are generally undervalued and underestimated.

However, with the right input, my child, and yours, can become all that they can be within the framework God has ordained for their lives. They can, and they will. I look forward to Jonathon's continued growth and development with great anticipation. I will invest in his life until there is no more life in me. At every opportunity, I will communicate to him that he is who God says he is. That's what I believe, and that is how it will be.

HOW CAN YOU HELP YOUR CHILD?

You can celebrate who your child is and what they do. You can let people know that your child is not incapacitated or incapable or any of the words that people use to describe and discriminate against people with disabilities. Reject the caveats that are put around your child that say because they're "learning disabled" they can't learn new skills. The truth is there are people who are labeled with learning disabilities who learn certain skills faster than those of us who are not labeled that way.

Give your child the same opportunities as a child who is not labeled with a learning disability. None of us knows what we are capable of until we are at least given an opportunity to try and be taught. So, teach your child how to do the best they can and be the best they can be. Every person has good in them, and everybody is able to become whoever they need to be because of who they are.

Invest the time, energy, and effort into your child's potential. Have a clear vision of who your child is rather than listening to the limits and boundaries that society puts around them. It's not down to teachers or carers. It's not down to doctors, psychiatrists, psychologists, or any other professional. It's down to you as a parent to decide how you want your child to be perceived. Fight to make sure your child is not treated like an outcast. Fight for their right to use their skills, talents, faculties, and whatever they have to learn to be a productive citizen in their own right. Help them achieve all they can achieve with the proper help, not tokenistic help. Have the highest expectations of your child, and continue to pour into their life.

I'm not here to try to convince you that this will be easy. It can be quite a hard road because you will likely be bombarded with negativity, and sometimes people won't understand or even be aware that they are being negative. Often, the way the "experts" will express things sounds like gloom and doom or throwing in the towel. You'll hear a lot of "this is how it is," and you may find yourself wondering *what can I do, and how can I help my child if everybody else sees them this way?* It can be an emotional roller-coaster, and sometimes you might feel like you want to scream at the world, *shut up!* Most times, you will be the only one standing on your child's side while everybody else is reeling off all the things your child cannot do because they are labeled learning disabled, are hearing impaired, or does not verbally express themself the way others do. But keep standing, come what may.

Interacting with Jonathon has been a pivotal part of my life. Having him in my life has been one of the most fulfilling things imaginable. It makes me smile to see the things he has been able to do and achieve, realizing that I play a part in helping him be the best he can be. I am committed to making sure he experiences life the best way he can experience it. He is my child. Therefore, whatever I have to give to him, I will give to the best of my ability.

I believe in Jonathon, and I see him through God's eyes. Looking at my child through God's eyes – through His wisdom, love, and care – strengthens the desires and dreams I have for Jonathon. He is seen as not like others, and although I want him to be treated like any other human being, I do not want him to be like others. He's his own individual, just as I am, just as my daughter is, just as my son is, and just as every individual is.

No one is like anyone else. We are all wonderfully unique and endowed with our several abilities. There is only one Jonathon in this world, no matter how many others bear the same name. No, he's not like the others, and I don't want him to be. I want him to be my child, his own person, and God's special creation. I want him to be himself. I want him to be who he is and to do the things that God has placed within him to do to the best of his ability.

The ignorance of society and even individuals who work in and around people with a diagnosis of learning disability is profound. The implications of this ignorance lead to wrong decisions being made, low outcomes, warped perceptions, and people diagnosed with a learning disability being treated as less than. Educating members of society with accurate information will change the mindset and achieve true equality for people with a learning disability diagnosis. A learning disability does not make someone ill, sick, contagious, totally vulnerable, useless, incapable, not good enough, or any of the myriad of labels placed on them from birth.

I speak on behalf of Jonathon and all those with this diagnosis: allow your child to thrive rather than having to constantly strive to be themselves. The status quo and archaic beliefs need to change surrounding disabilities, beginning with the word itself. They are not disabled. They are uniquely-abled. Today, I am the proud parent of a son who stands out as being different and unlike others in the eyes of society, and I would not have it any other way.

Jaime clutched his Woody and Buzz Lightyear toys, trying hard to string two words together to make a sentence. His school did not have much hope for his future because he was labeled "severely learning disabled." His behaviors were explosive, a response to all the pre-determined behaviors and self-fulfilling prophecies that had been spoken over his life. Jaime stumbled over himself when he walked and tried his best to show off who he was, but he was limited by what others said. He was sixteen years old.

The carers and service providers had high hopes, big dreams, and expected outcomes for Jaime. We conversed with him daily and told him how great he was and how much we expected him to achieve. We encouraged him, modeled what we expected, and gave him space to be the best version of himself, the best person God made him to be, with all his gifts and talents that shone beyond the dis-abilities. Jaime rose to the task and bowled us over, increasing in stature and wisdom, so much so that he was reading and writing fluently just five years later. He requires only minimal supervision and prompting in his daily life skills and holds a conversation with such eloquence and conviction that he can sway the listener to believe he has never struggled a day in his life.

How did Jaime go from a young adult with explosive behavior, labeled as severely disabled, to the highly functioning adult he is today? Those achievements came from being infused with big dreams and high hopes from people who believed that he was more than a label and what the school system said he was.

Abilities Development Ltd. was organically formed twelve years ago to realize the abilities beyond the disabilities of individuals who were condemned to a label for life. The sister company, Aspired Learning and Lifestyle Ltd., was formed two years ago to "pursue *all*" for people who are most vulnerable and marginalized because of what society says they cannot be or do.

Aspired Learning and Lifestyle was formed to change mindsets and help and inspire our vulnerable nation to aspire to become as independent as they possibly can be through regular mainstream activities that the rest of society takes for granted. We work with carers and support staff, professionals, and policymakers to transform their acceptance and support by renewing their minds about who our vulnerable individuals truly are.

Abilities Development offers programs of activities that stretch our young people and adults and shows them that they are part of the "everyone" Jesus came to earth for and that they are worthy, valuable, and belong. If you would like to receive more information about how we can help, visit our Abilities Development Ltd. website at www.abilitiesdevelopment.com.

ACKNOWLEDGMENTS

I am filled with gratitude for the incredible people who helped make this book a reality.

First and foremost, I would like to give honor to Yahweh, the one and only source of my strength, wisdom, and knowledge.

I must thank my sister, Carolene Hewitt, my trusted confidant, who offered her encouragement and time in reading the manuscript.

To my loving children, Kimberly and Stefan, words cannot express the depth of my gratitude for your unwavering support.

I want to thank my readers. You are the reason I write, and I hope this book will bring you as much contemplation and hope as it has brought me.

Finally, I want to thank the Winners publishing team for helping make my dream a reality. Special thanks to Aleathea Dupree, aka The Millionaire Writer, for bringing out the author in me and being absolutely phenomenal throughout the entire writing process.

ABOUT THE AUTHOR

Karen May, MSc., is a passionate and experienced educator and disabilities activist who currently serves as the Director of Abilities Development, where she uses her expertise to help individuals with cognitive impairments progress in life. She recently founded Aspired Learning and Lifestyle (ALL) to further the cause.

Born and raised in the West Indies, Karen is a mother of three. Her early experiences inspired and fueled her to become an advocate for individuals with cognitive impairments and to help them reach their full potential.

Karen is a highly qualified educator with a Bachelor's degree in Special Education, a Master's degree in International Teaching and Learning, and is currently pursuing her Doctorate in Special Education. She is recognized as a national leader in disabilities activism, thanks to her extensive knowledge and unwavering commitment to advocacy.

As Director of Abilities Development, Karen works tirelessly to ensure that individuals with cognitive impairments receive the support and resources they need to live fulfilling and productive lives. Under her leadership, Abilities Development has become a leading organization in its field, providing critical resources and support to individuals and families nationwide.

Karen's mission is to help families, professionals, and society at large understand and grow in their perception, interaction, expectations, and knowledge regarding individuals with cognitive impairments.

Connect with Karen at www.abilitiesdevelopment.com

www.ingramcontent.com/pod-product-compliance
Lightning Source LLC
Chambersburg PA
CBHW050752160726

48004CB00002B/532